Original title:
Beneath the Island Sky

Copyright © 2025 Creative Arts Management OÜ
All rights reserved.

Author: Maxwell Donovan
ISBN HARDBACK: 978-1-80581-587-7
ISBN PAPERBACK: 978-1-80581-114-5
ISBN EBOOK: 978-1-80581-587-7

Shadows of Paradise Revealed

A crab in a hurry, scuttles past,
Wearing a hat that's far too vast.
He waves at the seagulls, quite a sight,
Who steal his snack in a flappy flight.

Palm trees gossip, swaying with glee,
About the sunburned tourists, can't you see?
With sunscreen blobs that cover their toes,
They slip on their flip-flops, strike a pose.

The waves hide secrets, a fish in disguise,
In a funky bowtie and shiny pink ties.
He flops and he flails, trying to dance,
While nearby, a dolphin takes a chance.

The sandcastles crumble, a tide's cruel game,
As kids in the water shout out their name.
With buckets and shovels, they battle the sea,
A kingdom of laughter, wild and carefree.

Mirage of the Morning Sun

Seagulls squawk with morning cheer,
While I chase shadows, not quite here.
The toast is burnt, oh what a sight,
Coffee's dancing, just feels so right.

Palm trees wave, they tell me jokes,
As I untangle my beachy hoax.
The sunbeam slides right off my hat,
I trip on flip-flops, fancy that!

Where Silence Sings to the Stars

Underneath the patterned sky,
Crickets croon, don't be shy!
I hum a tune that's out of tune,
The moon just laughs, it's quite a boon.

Fireflies dance in silly glee,
Trying to sip my herbal tea.
Stars giggle down from heights above,
Can't blame them, they're born to love!

Lullabies of the Ocean Depths

Waves crash softly, tickling toes,
Starfish snicker where the seaweed grows.
The crab still plays his crabby game,
He snaps his claws, oh so lame!

Jellyfish wiggle in their blue,
While dolphins frolic, so fun to view.
I try to swim, but splash and flail,
And end up with seaweed in my tail!

The Colors of an Untouched Horizon

Sunset paints, a wild array,
I spill my drink, oh what a day!
Chasing hues of pink and gold,
While my ice cream melts, truth be told.

Clouds fluff up like cotton candy,
As I trip over my flip-flop handy.
The sky's a canvas, bright and bold,
But I'm just here, a sight to behold!

Reflections of Secrets in Tranquil Waters

Fish in fancy hats swim around,
Chasing lost treasures they have found.
With bubbles that pop, they giggle and cheer,
Whispering secrets, oh so unclear.

Crabs wearing flip-flops dance on the sand,
Telling tall tales of their grandband.
Seagulls with shades swoop down with style,
Making the beach a fashion trial.

The Allure of Hidden Harbors

Boats with beards bob like old men,
Complaining about how they've sailed again.
A parrot with jokes tires out the crew,
"Why did the seagull cross over to you?"

Buckets of lemonade sit on each pier,
Sipping while mermaids chime in with cheer.
They giggle and splash, creating a scene,
Alluring the fish with a dance so keen.

Nocturnal Serenades of the Shoreline

Under the stars, the crabs sing loud,
To a moonlit audience, quite proud.
With spoons in hand, they serve up a tune,
While the clumsy sea otter joins the festoon.

Glowworms giggle, lighting the path,
As jellyfish twirl, causing a laugh.
The night's a circus, a silly delight,
With waves whispering softly, 'All is right!'

The Embrace of the Evening Tide

Waves play tag with the sun's last light,
Tickling the toes of sandcastles bright.
A starfish winks, calling in the fun,
Oh! Look who's here, it's the crabby bun!

Laughter erupts as the tide pulls back,
Seashells gossip, no whispers they lack.
With chuckles and splashes, the evening proceeds,
Life at the shore is full of good deeds.

Moonlit Secrets of the Sandy Cove

The moon played tag with the sandy shore,
Crabs did the cha-cha, oh what a score!
Fish wore sunglasses, think they're so cool,
While turtles debate 'What's the best pool?'

Stars twinkled brightly, a cosmic ballet,
Seagulls complained, 'What a weird cabaret!'
A beach ball soared to the rhythm of fun,
While jellyfish grinned, 'We're still number one!'

Reflections in Azure Waters

In waters so blue, a fish took a dive,
Swimming in circles, said, 'I'm alive!'
Pelicans laughed, with beaks open wide,
While starfish conspired to cause a tide.

The sun winks down, giving all a grin,
As shrimp practice dance moves, none look like him.
The seaweed hums tunes, a watery song,
While otters roll over, just playing along!

The Dance of the Salted Air

Waves wiggled in rhythm, the shore shook with glee,
As seagulls strummed tunes on a salty spree.
Sandcastles giggled with sand-sculpted glee,
While crabs wore top hats, 'Tis a grand jubilee!

The air was a dancehall of fragrant delight,
With beach balls a-bouncin', what a funny sight!
A concert of laughter, with each ocean roar,
As dolphins played kazoo from a coral shore!

Secrets Guarded by Ancient Rocks

Old rocks told stories of pirates and gold,
But they chuckled and said, 'We're better off cold!'
Eels in tuxedos planned a grand soiree,
While clams whispered secrets, all night and day.

Octopus showed off with his stylish flair,
While a crab clapped hands, his dance was quite rare.
Echoes of laughter flew high in the air,
As the tide shared tales that none could compare!

Dreams among the Palms

In the shade of swaying trees,
The monkeys hide and tease their knees.
A crab on a mission, oh what a sight,
Wiggles sideways, trying with all its might.

The coconuts gossip up high and loud,
While birds practice singing to impress the crowd.
A lizard slips, takes a tumble, a funny fall,
Just another day with laughter for all.

Echoes of the Coral Reef

The fish have formed a conga line,
Dancing through bubbles, oh so divine.
A clam in the corner sings bold and strong,
With pearls for notes, it can't go wrong.

A turtle named Frank loves a bit of fun,
He tries to race, but he's slower than none.
The octopus juggles, with style and grace,
In this underwater circus, who can keep pace?

A Dance of Moonlit Tides

The moon winks down on a shrimp in a suit,
Who dances alone, oh, what a hoot!
Stars twinkle in rhythm, a cosmic cheer,
While the waves clap along, what a sight here!

A glowing jelly slides by with a grin,
Belting out tunes, she wants to win.
The sand crabs clap, creating a beat,
As the night comes alive, oh, what a treat!

Beneath Celestial Canopies

The coconuts giggle when the wind starts to blow,
As if sharing secrets that only they know.
A parrot declares, with feathers so bright,
That he's the king of this silly night!

Meanwhile, a sandcastle looks tall and proud,
Until a wave crashes, drawing a crowd.
"Who built this thing?" the tiny crabs shout,
As they scurry away, filled with doubt!

Journeys in the Twilight Seas

On a boat made of cheese,
With a crew of dancing bees,
We sailed through jelly waves,
In search of pie-shaped caves.

The captain wore a hat,
Made of butter and a cat,
He claimed he knew the way,
To find the land of sway.

The fish all juggled cards,
While seagulls played guitars,
We laughed until we cried,
With our goofy nautical pride.

When the stars began to twirl,
And the waves began to whirl,
We anchored in a dream,
Where silly things could gleam.

The Language of the Salted Air

In a world where whispers play,
The wind told jokes all day,
Seashells giggled with delight,
Under the moon's silly light.

The sand said, "How do you do?"
As the waves wore socks of blue,
Crabs danced with a funny flair,
In the language of the air.

A parrot squawked with sass,
While we sipped from a glass,
Of lemonade that sparkled bright,
With a twist of giggles in the night.

Among the clouds so puffy, fun,
We laughed till we saw the sun,
As the tide tickled our toes,
In the breeze, the perfect prose.

Passionate Hues in the Evening Sky

As the sun said its goodbye,
The colors made us sigh,
With shades that winked and winked,
And painted clouds that blinked.

The pinks and purples danced,
While the blues hopped and pranced,
We wore hats made of rays,
And marveled at their plays.

A flamingo on a swing,
Sang songs of silly things,
With a ukulele bright,
They serenaded the night.

Under this laughter's hue,
The world felt fresh and new,
With giggles as our guide,
In the twilight, we would glide.

The Tangle of Roots and Stars

Roots of trees twisted tight,
Whispering secrets at night,
While the stars played hide-and-seek,
In a game that felt so cheek.

The moon wore a funny grin,
As the owls joined in the din,
They hooted jokes, oh what a sight,
In the tangled, starry light.

We climbed up the branches high,
And waved at clouds passing by,
With a squirrel juggling nuts,
And a raccoon in cute struts.

Amidst the roots and leaves,
Were laughter and silly thieves,
Stealing joy from night's embrace,
In this merry, magical place.

The Enchantment of Coral Gardens

In the depths where fish can laugh,
Coral castles have a giraffe.
Turtles dance with mighty grace,
While starfish play in a slow race.

Seashells gossip, tales unfold,
Bubbles burst with secrets bold.
Anemones throw a wild bash,
Where clowns swim in a quirky clash.

Treasure chests of pirate's dreams,
Filled with jelly and funny schemes.
Octopus serves drinks with flair,
As seahorses twirl without a care.

In this realm, all worries cease,
Where laughter floats, and joy's a feast.
Coral gardens, shine and sway,
The ocean's charm, in a playful display.

Underneath the Aurora of Waves

Jellyfish glow in rainbow hues,
Dancing like they've drunk the booze.
Crabs pinch with a comic twist,
While mermaids laugh, they can't resist.

Seaweed sways, much like a wig,
Fish in outfits do a jig.
Stars above and shells below,
Offer jokes that make us glow.

Surfers ride on bubbles bold,
In a world that's bright and gold.
Seals serenade with a croon,
As dolphins play beneath the moon.

Waves roll in with a cheerful clap,
Each splash tells a funny chap.
Underneath, a show of glee,
In waters deep, there's mystery.

The Colors of Dusk at Sea

As the sun dips down with glee,
The fish wave bye, "Come dance with me!"
Clouds wear pink, like cotton candy,
While a grouper's face looks quite dandy.

The horizon bursts in orange blaze,
With pirate ships that strut and gaze.
Seagulls squawk their funny song,
In every note, they can't go wrong.

Twilight brings a magic show,
Where polka-dots are all aglow.
A whale plays hide and seek with flair,
As shrimps line up, with jokes to share.

Undercover, the night begins,
With crabs telling notorious sins.
In the colors of dusk so neat,
The ocean giggles, oh so sweet.

Secrets Lurking Under the Surface

A clam hides secrets in its shell,
Whispers tales, it knows quite well.
Octopuses plot in clever schemes,
While seahorses giggle at their dreams.

Starfish swap stories, oh so sly,
While urchins pretend to be shy.
In coral nooks, the secrets keep,
As fish share jokes beneath the deep.

The current flows with a playful grin,
It teases crabs with a sly spin.
Eels play peek-a-boo with a twist,
In this dance of the ocean mist.

So listen close, for laughter's near,
In the depths where all is clear.
Secrets laugh, they bounce and weave,
In a world where jesters never leave.

Mysterious Currents of the Night

Moonlight dances on the sea,
Crabs are grooving, wild and free.
Fish wear hats, they all agree,
To hold a party, just for me!

Stars are laughing, flickering bright,
Seahorses twirl, what a sight!
Turtles tell jokes with all their might,
The ocean's mischief brings delight!

Serenade of the Whispering Waves

Waves are singing tunes of cheer,
Shells are clapping, lend an ear.
Gulls joke about the fish they fear,
While dolphins dance, their path is clear!

Octopus bands play on the sly,
With silly hats, oh my, oh my!
A sea breeze whispers, 'give it a try,'
As laughter echoes from nearby!

Fragments of Dreams on Sunlit Shores

On sunny sands, dreams run amok,
Kites fly high, and seashells rock.
Sandy toes and a sandman's clock,
The beach is a stage, a jester's flock!

Seagulls steal fries, what a fuss!
While kids giggle, make a plus.
With ice cream drips and a splash, a rush,
Laughter rides the waves we trust!

Love Songs in the Salty Breeze

The breeze hums sweet, a tune so bright,
Couples dance by the moon's soft light.
With lovebirds perched and hearts in flight,
A conch shell plays, it feels just right!

Sandy hearts shaped with glee,
Whispers echo, 'come dance with me.'
A clumsy crab makes his plea,
Even fish share love, can't you see?

The Heart of the Tropical Night

Crickets sing with wild guile,
A lizard dances, all in style.
Coconuts fall with a gentle thud,
While palms sway, lost in the mud.

The moon has a party, candles bright,
As stars wear their fanciest light.
A parrot laughs, but what a bore,
Could he find jokes that we adore?

The drinks are flowing, mishaps too,
I tripped on a flip-flop, oh what a view!
The tide rolls in, a soft embrace,
Making sandcastles fall from grace.

Floating dreams in coconut shells,
Mermaids giggle with their spells.
The night winds whisper tales of fun,
Where laughter sparkles, everyone runs.

A Harmony of Dusk and Dawn

As shadows dance and colors clash,
A rooster crows with quite a splash.
Tropical fruit falls from the trees,
While monkeys tease in a playful breeze.

The sun waves goodbye, all aglow,
Rabbits in tuxedos steal the show!
Pineapples in punny discussions,
While bananas make softer cushions.

Clouds turn pink with a cheeky grin,
As iguanas join the morning din.
Flip-flops flop with a funky sound,
In this paradise where joy is found.

Tides tickle toes, laughter will rule,
Nature's own circus, oh what a fool!
Lighthearted breezes sweep us away,
Creating mischief as we play.

Vibrations of a Forgotten Paradise

Old palm trees sport eccentric hats,
As seagulls conduct the choir of chats.
A hammock sways, taking a leap,
While island dreams bubble, never sleep.

Jellyfish waltz in the shallow tide,
With surfboards getting caught in their ride.
Crabs hold court, the judges so stern,
While seaweed swirls in its twisted turn.

A conch shell speaks, pretending to know,
Secrets of shells, oh, what a show!
Starfish wear socks or so they say,
Grinning wide, they dance the day.

The sun finally dips, twilight's embrace,
As the waves giggle in a playful chase.
Find your joy in this wacky view,
In an earthy party where fun is true!

Silhouettes at Dusk

The horizon blushes, an evening tease,
Lizards prance 'round, deftly with ease.
Fishermen whisper their evening plans,
While crabs hold court with their tiny fans.

Coconuts roll like boulders that dare,
While turtles trot with a casual flair.
Evening gown flowers open wide,
Waving their petals with daring pride.

The last rays of sunlight play peek-a-boo,
As shadows recite their own funny hue.
Waves tickle toes, a bubbly affair,
As fireflies dance, bursting with flair.

Oh, laughter echoes beneath the dusk,
Where playful dreams are a must.
In this quirky world of colors ablaze,
We find delight in the most fanciful ways.

Soliloquies of the Harbor Night

In the harbor where fish swim,
A bird yells, 'It's me or him!'
The moon laughs at the scene,
As sailors sip their caffeine.

A crab scuttles with great glee,
Chasing dreams beneath the sea.
A rubber duck floats by,
Quacking loud at the starry sky.

The lighthouse winks and spins,
While spooky tales begin.
The waves dance with the shore,
Who knew nights could be such a chore?

And as the night drifts on by,
The sea otters wave, oh my!
Bubbles pop like giggling sprites,
In this harbor of starry nights.

A Glimpse of Endless Blue

The ocean laughs with a roar,
While gulls squawk, wanting more.
A fish jumps high for a joke,
And lands on a sleepy bloke.

Seashells whisper to the breeze,
"Catch us if you can, oh please!"
As kids dive with a splash,
Creating mayhem in a flash.

The sun wears sunglasses blissfully,
While sandcastles stand so mischievously.
Laughter rings from every shore,
Entrancing all who dare explore.

And when the day starts to close,
Jellyfish strike a funny pose.
With a giggle and a cheer,
The endless blue brings us near.

Island Echoes in the Stillness

Whispers float on a gentle breeze,
As turtles dance, feeling at ease.
Coconuts giggle, hanging tight,
In the quiet glow of twilight.

A parrot jokes about the sun,
Saying, "Where's that shade? I'm done!"
Seashells clap as they lay,
Sharing secrets of the day.

A crab sings in a too-high key,
Causing fish to roll in glee.
The palm trees sway with a grin,
While waves play tag, wanting to win.

As night drapes its velvet cloak,
Stars laugh at the island folk.
Echoes of joy softly blend,
In stillness where fun has no end.

Veiled by the Embrace of Stars

Stars twinkle, wearing hats of light,
While owls hoot, preparing for flight.
A firefly lands on a sleepy cat,
And gives it a shout, "You're too fat!"

The night creatures come out to play,
While crickets chirp, making their way.
Moonbeams dance on the ocean's face,
As jellybeans roll in jubilant race.

Fishing boats sing with a swish,
While dolphins leap for a splashy wish.
The seaweed waves as if to say,
"Keep dancing here, come what may!"

So with stars shining high above,
This night shows just how to love.
For under this cosmic blanket, oh dear,
Laughter and joy bring us near.

Light Beyond the Jade Waters

In a land where fish wear hats,
And crabs dance in silly spats,
The sun laughs on the ocean's edge,
While seaweed sways in sea's hedge.

A dolphin lost its sense of style,
With sunglasses on, it swam a mile.
Gulls gossip about the tide,
While turtles chat, their shells their pride.

The starfish chill with ice cream scoops,
Offering flavors to passing troops.
Each wave brings a new surprise,
As laughter echoes, brightens the skies.

With coral reefs, the playground calls,
Where jellyfish play in summer brawls.
They bounce and giggle in ocean's sway,
Life's a party, come join the play!

The Allure of Starlit Retreats

Under lights that twinkle and tease,
Laughter flows with the gentle breeze.
A crab dressed in a shiny bow tie,
Declares it's time for the limbo, oh my!

The moon dips low with a cheeky grin,
As we twirl and spin, let the fun begin.
A seagull steals a potato chip,
We chase it down, not a single slip.

Bamboozled by a playful tide,
Mermaids giggle and take a ride.
With buckets of joy, we scoop and play,
The stars wink down on our merry fray.

As jellyfish join our midnight dance,
We float and drift in a sea of chance.
With every splash, we shout with glee,
In this starlit realm, forever carefree!

Notes from the Quiet Bay

In a bay where froggy frogs croak songs,
The hermit crabs wear the silliest throngs.
The anchovies swim with curious glee,
As playful otters join in the spree.

A turtle sings off-key by a tree,
While fish chuckle in perfect harmony.
Seashells gossip about a fishy tale,
Of a snail who tried to use the mail.

The waves giggle under the bright sun,
As jellybeans bounce, oh what fun!
Each splash brings laughter, a joyous sound,
In this quiet bay, where fun's always found.

The breeze winks gently, tickles the sand,
And we can't help but clap our hands.
With each wave's whisper, joy takes flight,
As we dance together in pure delight!

Murmurs of the Twilight Coast

At twilight's edge, where shadows play,
The crickets chirp a funny ballet.
A starfish mime performs on the sand,
While sea turtles join in, a funny band.

Lighthouses blink with a giggling light,
Guiding fish home, all snug and tight.
As surging waves burst into a cheer,
We laugh till dusk, our worries clear.

The sea sponge rolls in to crack a joke,
While sandcastles wobble, and then provoke.
With every giggle, the tide rolls high,
Tickling our toes, oh me, oh my!

In a world where the ocean's shy laugh flows,
We dance on the shores, where joy always grows.
With every dawn, a promise anew,
More funny moments waiting for you!

Serenade of the Sea Breeze

The seagulls squawk and dive,
Pinching fries from tourists' hands.
The waves whisper silly jokes,
While clams throw sand in the bands.

Sandy toes dance with delight,
As crabs wear hats made of seaweed.
A beach ball rolls past a kite,
While sunburned folks attempt to plead.

Surfboards crash in a fine thrash,
Mermaids giggle in the swell.
Sun-tanned friends enjoy a splash,
While jellyfish juggle as well.

As the sun sets over the bay,
A dolphin leaps in a grin.
It's all a wacky display,
Where every laugh is a win.

The Hidden Heart of Paradise

In a hut made of coconut shells,
A parrot mimics the news.
The palm trees gossip like old pals,
Sharing tales of flip-flop blues.

Tanned tourists lose their way,
Chasing shadows of a sand crab.
While local kids laugh at play,
Thinking adults are just mad.

A treasure map drawn on a napkin,
Leads to a stash of melted ice.
X marks the spot by the napkin,
Where pineapples roll, oh so nice!

As sunset paintbrushes the sky,
Laughter burbles like light rain.
With every sunset, time floats by,
We'll do it all again, insane.

Murmurs of Forgotten Beaches

Lost flip-flops line the shore,
As beach balls bounce with delight.
A coconut falls with a roar,
Hitting a hammock in flight.

Sandy kids build castles tall,
While a crab declares his throne.
Sunscreen splatters like a brawl,
As sunburnt kings make it known.

The tide brings in seaweed strands,
That tickle tourists' sun-kissed toes.
While everyone claps, "More bands!"
For the band that sings, well, who knows?

Under a pineapple tree,
Laughter echoes all around.
Every moment feels so free,
With joy, warmth, and joy abound.

Fragments of Salt and Sand

A bucket spills tons of shells,
As toddlers hunt for a prize.
Lucky finds in sandy swells,
Baking under the bright skies.

Picnic baskets burst at seams,
As ants stage their grand parade.
Kites swoop low, they swerve in dreams,
While burger flames begin to fade.

Tanning oils clash with the sun,
As laughter floats on the breeze.
Not a worry, everyone's won,
While flip-flops make silly sneeze.

Under a sky painted gold,
Even time laughs and stands still.
These memories glimmer, bold,
In the heart, they always will.

The Tides of Forgotten Dreams

The sun sets bright, it's a wild affair,
Seagulls squawking without a care.
The beach ball rolls, they chase with glee,
While sandcastles crumble, oh what a spree!

Flip-flops flying, a dog steals a snack,
Kids building towers, but where's the snack pack?
Laughter erupts, the ocean's our friend,
With sunscreen on noses, the fun will not end.

The tide dances back, playing a game,
As crabs do a jig, oh such silly fame.
Surfboards wobble, we glide and we fall,
This beach day of whimsy, let's treasure it all!

In waves of giggles, we soak up the cheer,
With friends by our side, there's nothing to fear.
The tides may roll in, but our spirits won't fade,
In turns of fun moments, sweet memories made!

Celestial Secrets Over Coral Shores

Stars twinkle down on the frothy blue,
Whispers of dolphins, do they hear us too?
With buckets and shovels, we dig down quite deep,
Finding old treasures, or just some sea creep!

The moon's a big cheese, we laugh at its sight,
Our beachside dance party goes late into night.
With ukuleles strumming a goofy old tune,
Sand slipping through fingers beneath the soft moon.

The tide tries to steal our snacks for the show,
As we dodge waves, full of giggles and glow.
A crab in a cap joins our beach jubilee,
What a funny sight, oh what glee we see!

The sea's our stage, the stars do confide,
Tales of sandy shenanigans tossed on the tide.
In this realm of laughter, we sing and we soar,
A night full of secrets forever explore!

Echoes of the Distant Waves

Waves crashing softly, they call and they tease,
Shells filled with stories, a crasher in the breeze.
With laughter as loud as a seagull's bold cry,
The sand holds our secrets and dreams that won't die.

A bucket of sand, with hiccuping glee,
We sing to the ocean, oh can't you see?
The tide rolls in fast, wearing a big grin,
As we tumble and rumble, let the fun begin!

Frothy waves splash, a giggle parade,
While fish in the sea just roll their eyes, played!
We build silly monsters, our castle ascent,
A fortress of joy, why's the tide so bent?

With beach balls and umbrellas all out of line,
We sketch in the sand, our goofiest design.
Echoes of laughter, sweet songs of delight,
In a dance with the waves, we're stars of the night!

The Heartbeat of Hidden Shores

At dawn's early light, the surf starts to hum,
Watch out, here come the marshmallow bum!
Flip-flops encounter a crab with a grin,
Chasing the waves as they wince and spin.

Sandy shenanigans lead to a splash,
In our quest for treasures, we move with a dash.
The jellyfish giggles as we run by fast,
Dashing through troubles, our worries won't last!

Picnics of snacks, oh what a delight,
Too much jelly, a sticky old sight!
Seashells are gathering tales of our fun,
As we wave back to the ocean, our own number one.

With laughter and bubbles, the heart beats anew,
The shores of our stories, forever in view.
In a whirl of beach games, we dance 'round the day,
Every moment together, hip-hip-hooray!

The Solitude of Whispered Breezes

The wind told secrets, soft and sly,
It teased my hat and made it fly.
A tree giggled when I passed by,
I waved it back, oh, don't be shy!

Clouds rolled like laughter in the air,
I chased one down without a care.
It turned and played hide-and-seek,
With sunshine's rays, quite cheek to cheek.

A squirrel joined me on the quest,
With acorn snacks, we were the best!
Together we plotted a grand scheme,
To catch the breeze—a silly dream!

So off we went, our giggles gleamed,
In a world where nothing seemed,
To matter much but fun and play,
We danced with whispers through the day.

Dreams Cast by Starry Nights

Stars twinkled like winking bugs,
I laid on grass, feeling all snug.
The moon wore shades, looked quite cool,
While frogs held court in the moonlit pool.

The milky way danced with silly glee,
A cosmic ballet, oh what a spree!
Aliens giggled, played tag with beams,
While I tried to count all my dreams.

A comet zoomed by, said, "Catch my tail!"
I threw a wish, oh please don't fail!
But it just laughed and sped away,
To find another starry play.

So I drifted off, full of delight,
With dreams of capers till morning light.
And when I woke, I felt so spry,
Still dancing under that twinkling sky.

The Lure of Ceaseless Mysteries

A treasure map made of jello slice,
Led me to giggles, more than once or thrice.
X marked the spot, but it turned out to be,
A picnic with ants who begged for tea.

Waves chatted secrets to the shore,
As crabs performed a tap dancing score.
I tried to join, but slipped on sand,
Only to find a jellyfish band.

The stars above whispered back and forth,
"Who would have thought of this quirk's worth?"
I laughed so much, my cheeks turned bright,
Joining the creatures in the starlit night.

In the end, the mysteries were clear,
That laughter and fun are always near.
For every challenge or puzzle in tow,
Find the joke, let joy freely flow.

Navigation of the Cosmic Waters

With a rubber duck, I sailed the space,
Through cosmic waters, I found my place.
Stars were my crew, with a wink and a grin,
Colorful fish danced, let the fun begin!

Galaxies spun like cotton candy,
I tried to catch one, it felt so dandy.
Each twinkling splash was a giggle and cheer,
In this vast ocean, there was nothing to fear.

A whale blew bubbles, shaped like pies,
While octopuses played with sticky ties.
I joined their game, a vast cosmic tease,
Weathered the waves with the greatest of ease.

As I navigated through laughter's tide,
With my trusty duck as captain and guide.
I found that adventure, no matter how far,
Always sails best with a joyful star.

Echoes of Legends in the Breeze

The parrot sings tales of old,
While crabs dance in the sand so bold.
Laughter floats on salty air,
Mermaids giggle, but do they care?

The coconut falls with a clunk,
Islanders think it's pure junk.
But gather 'round for stories grand,
Of treasure buried deep in sand!

A turtle races, oh so slow,
While fish take bets on the show.
The waves keep whispering their tune,
As seagulls argue with the moon.

With every gust, a joke is spun,
Unearthed laughter, pure island fun!
So raise a drink, let joy grow wide,
In the ocean's silly tide.

The Gentle Hand of Time on Paradise

Time tickles palms like playful breeze,
Swaying between bright coconuts trees.
The sun slips slowly, wearing its hat,
While crabs hold council, quite round and flat.

The clock is a hammock, swaying with glee,
Forget the minutes, drink coconut tea!
Sandy footprints lead joyfully,
As dolphins grin at what they see.

The gentle waves, they shuffle and slide,
Urging us to join the ride.
With every tick, a joke unfurls,
As laughter rolls in, swirls and twirls.

So let the hours do their dance,
Life's a party, let's take a chance!
Under the stars, merriment flows,
With breezy tales that everyone knows.

Traces of Stars on Wavy Waters

Stars flip-flop on the rolling tide,
Wiggling like fish on a summer ride.
The moon dons shades, looking quite cool,
As dolphins splash, they break the rule.

The sea laughs loudly, tickling the night,
As jellyfish glow, a whimsical sight.
In this dance where joys collide,
The waves invite all to join the ride.

An octopus sneezes, causing a stir,
While seagulls attempt to dance but prefer a slur.
All the fish join the cosmic dance,
Stars above giggle at their chance.

Under the shimmer, secrets abound,
As laughter echoes, bond is found.
With every splash, another jest,
In the water's heart, we find our zest.

Sunrise over Ghostly Shores

Ghosts of sandcastles, once proud and tall,
Now play with shadows, do they recall?
The sun rises up, providing a show,
As sleepy seashells wink to and fro.

The breeze whispers secrets, a mischievous tease,
Stirring up laughter with effortless ease.
As sunrise paints skies in shades of delight,
Even the ghosts can't resist the bright light.

Waves crash gently, like snores of the night,
While crabs join in, hopping left, then right.
Mirth erupts like foam on the crest,
Amongst these shores, who knows what's best?

With each dawn, hilarity wakes,
As sun-drenched mischief the shoreline shakes.
The laughter of spirits fills the air,
In reignited joy, we all share.

The Pulse of the Coral Lagoon

Fish wear suits, they swim in style,
Crabs hold meetings with a wacky smile.
Sea turtles gossip, tales they weave,
Underwater parties, you won't believe!

Jellyfish dance like they're on a spree,
With disco lights, so wild and free.
The clownfish crack jokes, a real delight,
While octopuses juggle, what a sight!

Seashells gossip by the sandy dunes,
While starfish strut to their own tunes.
The waves applaud, oh what a show,
In the coral lagoon, laughter will flow!

A dolphin dives with a playful flip,
Anemones smile, they don't even trip.
Underwater giggles fill the air,
Joy is abundant, everywhere!

Canvas of the Setting Sun

The sun paints colors, a brush in the sky,
While seagulls squabble, oh my, oh my!
Pirate parrots squawk with glee,
Stealing snacks from a careless bee!

Sandy toes wiggle, dancing around,
As shells gossip, the funniest sound.
The horizon swells, a curious plot,
Where mermaids plot mischief — oh what a lot!

Crabs in tuxedos, looking so grand,
Hold a soirée on the warm, soft sand.
Starfish serve drinks, oh what a treat,
While kids chase waves, skipping on feet!

Sunset's laughter, in colors bright,
As twilight sneaks in, painting the night.
The best magic show, for all to behold,
The canvas of sun sets, a sight to unfold!

Solace in the Island Breeze

The palm trees giggle, swaying in line,
As the coconut clowns play fetch with sunshine.
Kids chase rainbows that flutter near,
While ice cream drips and laughter's clear!

Tropical birds dress up for a ball,
With feathers so bright, they dazzle us all.
Lizards wearing hats, oh what a tease,
Basking in warmth, enjoying the breeze!

Waves send whispers of silly tales,
Of underwater pranks and gusty gales.
The sunset nods, giving a wink,
As night emerges, it's time to drink!

Fireflies dance like a twinkling show,
While laughter erupts in a playful flow.
The island hums with a cheerful tease,
In the solace found, oh what a breeze!

Horizon's Edge of Mystery

Where the sea meets the sky, funny things happen,
Like dolphins in suits, who love to start clappin'.
The horizon leans close, curious to peek,
At the jellyfish jokes that make the waves squeak!

Clouds drift by, sharing silly dreams,
Of mermaids who twirl in sparkly streams.
With seashells chuckling, they all conspire,
To tease the sun until it's on fire!

The sand becomes canvas, where footprints play,
With silly shapes that giggle all day.
Seagulls make faces, wise and absurd,
While fish write poems, their voices unheard!

At dusk, the horizon whispers a jest,
A riddle perhaps, can you guess the best?
In this land of mystery, fun never fades,
Where laughter is painted in bright periwades!

The Lure of Twilight Waters

The fish wear tiny hats, I swear,
They hold a dance with quite the flair,
Twirling beneath the stars' bright lights,
As crabs play drums on sandy nights.

The mermaids gossip, tails all a-twirl,
Sharing secrets in a whirling whirl,
While sea turtles race in a slow crawl,
And seagulls laugh at it all—what a ball!

The waves hum tunes to sleepy stars,
Jellyfish twinkle like tiny cars,
We'd join in, but we've lost our shoes,
Splashing in laughter, what could we lose?

So, come for a swim, don't take a nap,
Let's catch the sunset in a fishy trap,
With all this fun, how can one stay dry?
We'll be pristine until the sun's goodbye!

Enchanted by Island Mist

The fog waltzes in with a playful grin,
Hiding coconuts like cheeky kin,
Parrots giggle, rustling the trees,
While monkeys swing, aiming to please.

Drifting on air, the mist is a tease,
Catching the birds that come with the breeze,
It tickles our noses, makes us sneeze loud,
While we dance together, lost in the crowd.

A crab in a tux struts across the sand,
His dance so fine, isn't it grand?
The fish wear sunglasses and throw a bash,
The party's a blast, let's make a splash!

So, lose your worries, let's take a chance,
Join the rhythm of an island dance,
Wrapped in mist, let laughter unroll,
What's life without fun? It feeds the soul!

Reflections on a Velvet Wave

A wave races in, all silky and sly,
It tickles my toes—oh my, oh my!
With splashes of laughter under the moon,
The ocean sings us a bubbly tune.

Starlit echoes bounce off the shore,
As fish throw a party, and who could ignore?
They wear little crowns, call each other king,
While shells cheer loudly, "Let's dance and sing!"

The rhythm of waves, like a swaying drum,
Makes everyone dance, even the glum.
A crab on a skateboard, what a sight,
Rolling past us, giggling with delight.

So let's ride the curls of this oceanic fun,
With laughter as bright as the morning sun,
For moments like these, oh so surreal,
Make the waves dance, that's the biggest deal!

Imaginations in the Tropical Twilight

As twilight creeps with a silly face,
We build castles of sand in this playful place,
Seashells whisper secrets, or so they claim,
While we craft stories in this whimsical game.

An octopus juggles, it's quite a sight,
While starfish cheer with all of their might,
The tide rolls in with a playful wave,
And everyone here feels fancy and brave.

Bananas in pajamas float on by,
Joined by turtles who soar and fly,
Underneath palms that sway like a band,
We sing ocean ballads, all unplanned.

So grab your friends, let's be a bit wild,
Join in the fun, let laughter be styled,
For as the sun dips down from the sky,
We'll dance under stars, waving worries goodbye!

Twilight Tales of a Hidden Cove

In a cove where crabs wear hats,
And fish gossip like old chitchat,
The seaweed dances with the tide,
While turtles giggle, wide-eyed.

A clam sings opera, oh so grand,
As starfish cheer and take a stand.
The moonlight bathes the scene just right,
Where laughter echoes through the night.

But oh, the seagulls steal the show,
With prankish antics, row by row.
They swoop and dive, a feathery fleet,
While dolphins dive with flippant feet.

So sip your coconut with glee,
Join in the laughter, wild and free.
The hidden cove, a comical sight,
Where twilight tales bring pure delight.

Ocean's Cradle at Dusk.

As the sun dips low, the waves all cheer,
A clam in shades sips salty beer.
Fish play poker in a coral nook,
While squids publish their own funny book.

In the cradle of waves so soft,
A jellyfish dances, swaying aloft.
Octopuses juggle with flair and grace,
As barnacles chuckle at slow-paced race.

The sailboats wave like they know a joke,
While flip-flops fly from a silly bloke.
The ocean's cradle rocks with laughter,
As sea life plays, chasing ever after.

So as dusk settles and stars appear,
Join the hullabaloo, shed your fear.
For in this cradle, pure cheer will reign,
In a world where humor's the main domain.

Whispers of the Seabreeze

The seabreeze carries soft-spoken pranks,
As pelicans dance on slippery planks.
Whispers of waves tickle the shore,
While fish toss jokes and ask for more.

A crab plays tag with a sneaky shoe,
While dolphins splash, making hullabaloo.
The whispering breeze sings gentle tunes,
As clowns in the ocean wear funny balloons.

Yet, look close at the hermit's new shell,
It's the cookie jar where secrets dwell.
Surprise awaits with every gust,
As laughter bubbles, a joyful must.

So breathe in deep the salty air,
Join the whispers, the jokes to share.
In this seaside kingdom full of jest,
The seabreeze brings mirth and a spirit of fest.

Shadows Beneath the Palm Trees

In the shadows, where the coconuts sway,
A monkey grins, ready to play.
With a wink and a twist, he swings with glee,
While palm fronds flutter, inviting the spree.

Lizards wear glasses, reading the news,
While crabs kick back in snazzy shoes.
The shadows grow long, laughter erupt,
As goofy sea turtles tumble and sup.

Beneath the palms, the parties ignite,
With glow-in-the-dark fish lighting the night.
Their jokes ripple out like waves in the sea,
Creating a symphony of humor and glee.

So join the fun in the moonlit arc,
Where shadows bring laughter, igniting a spark.
In this palm tree realm of laughs and fun,
Every dusk promises jokes just begun.

Stars Drifting Over Turquoise Waters

On a boat made of laughter and dreams,
Fish wear sunglasses, or so it seems.
Jellyfish dancing to the sea's great song,
They invite all the turtles to come sing along.

Crabs in a conga line under a moonbeam,
They've got moves that'll make you want to scream!
Seagulls are gossiping up in the breeze,
Trading old tales, as they feast on some cheese.

The waves laugh loud, tickling the shore,
They play hide-and-seek with flip-flops galore.
Stars are winking, adding to the jest,
Who knew the ocean could throw such a fest?

And as the night drapes its shimmering gown,
I spot a mermaid who's lost her crown.
With a splash and a giggle, she takes a bow,
The ocean's a party; come join us now!

The Poetry of the Quiet Coastline

The quiet coast whispers secrets at night,
Where seaweed sings softly, all feels just right.
Shells tell their stories, each one unique,
While crabs practice yoga, it's quite the peak.

A lighthouse winks as if telling a joke,
While fishermen dream on their floating cloak.
Tides play charades with the gulls overhead,
While sandcastles mourn that their builders have fled.

Dolphins giggle, leaping with flair,
Taking windsurfing lessons, oblivious to care.
In the distance, a clam shimmies in glee,
As he rolls in the surf to the rhythm of three.

Just a glance at the ocean, and you'll find,
That silliness flourishes in waves—purely divine.
In the realm of the surf, with the sun dipping low,
Life's perfect distraction is just letting go.

Embracing the Twilight Tide

The sunset giggles with orange and pink,
Mermaids take selfies and sip from the sink.
Oysters are rapping, while dolphins beatbox,
As starfish thumb-wrestle on their sandy blocks.

The sky blushes bright, a playful charade,
While the tide rolls in with a wave serenade.
Octopuses juggle, while crabs eat popcorn,
Oh, what a sight 'til the break of dawn!

Turtles paint rainbows with brushes so wide,
As they dive in the sea for a fun water slide.
With a flip and a splash, they make quite a scene,
In this wacky wave wonderland, all feels like a dream.

As stars start to twinkle, the fun's not done,
For the sea holds secrets of laughter and run.
The night calls us forth, with a chuckle so bright,
In the arms of the tide, our spirits take flight!

Beneath the Sugarloaf Skies

Where cotton candy clouds drift and swirl,
Pineapple drinks make the sea breeze twirl.
Fish pull pranks on the passing boats,
While turtles tune up their sweet vocal notes.

Balloons float by with a giggle or two,
As jellybeans twinkle in waters so blue.
Seagulls host tea parties with delicate grace,
While otters make ruckus at a slow-motion race.

The sunset's a circus, a color parade,
Even the seaweed has joined in the trade.
With bubbles and laughter escaping each wave,
We find joy in nature, oh how it behaves!

As night brushes softly with stars that align,
The ocean sings sweet nothings, divine.
In this joyful embrace of the twilight glow,
The magic of laughter is ours to bestow.

The Call of the Gentle Surf

Waves tickle toes in playful jest,
Shells chuckle loud, they know best.
Seagulls squawk with feathered flair,
While crabs dance like they haven't a care.

Sun hats fly, a breeze the thief,
Dune buggies zoom, startling the reef.
Beach umbrellas tip in glee,
As sunscreen battles an army of sand, oh me!

Laughter spills like water bright,
Flip-flops caught in the twilight's light.
Even fish are laughing too,
As they sneak up on unsuspecting shoe.

With giggles echoing far and wide,
A day at sea is a sweetened ride.
So come, dear friend, join the fun,
Under the sun, the laughter's begun.

Shimmering Shadows at Sundown

Coconuts sway with a cheeky grin,
As shadows stretch, the fun begins.
The sunset blushes, oh what a sight,
While crickets start their evening light.

Flip-flops squeak a silly song,
As beachgoers dance, and silliness throngs.
Tiki torches flicker, casting odd shapes,
While everyone swaps funny landscape grapes.

With every splash, a laugh erupts,
From sandcastle kings, hilarious pups.
Even the stars are up for the game,
As jellyfish glow, calling out names.

So toast to the dusk, with coconut cheer,
With funny tales of the day, oh dear!
Let shadows twirl in the warm, bright glow,
For beneath this sunset, laughter will flow.

Constellations Over Eternal Sands

The stars gossip in a twinkling spree,
While sand crabs plot their destiny.
Moonbeams laugh, casting silly sights,
As galaxies crack jokes all night.

Tired turtles stretch in slow-motion dance,
Finding their groove in a starry trance.
Shooting stars dart, a raucous flight,
As people ponder, 'Is that a fish or a kite?'

With every grunt from the ocean bed,
The salty breeze whispers giggles instead.
Distant islands chuckle, keeping score,
While mermaids roll their eyes at the shore.

As laughter mingles with the ocean's sigh,
We raise our voices, and together we cry.
In this cosmic jest of the night sky,
Let's keep the laughter, oh me, oh my!

The Breath of the Coral Reefs

Tickling fish in a swirling dance,
Coral castles give a playful glance.
Octopuses giggle through their masks,
While seaweed waves as it happily basks.

Bubble-blowers have a bubbly dream,
In the underwater world, the bubbles beam.
Anemones laugh, their colors provide,
As clownfish swim with a comical pride.

With every ripple, a chuckle flows,
Seashells hide treasures, and secrets they know.
So dive on in, the water's all right,
Where laughter and bubbles are quite the sight.

In coral gardens where silliness reigns,
The ocean's heart beats with joy and gains.
Join the dance, feel the flippered glee,
For in every wave, there's a giggle, you see!

Journeys through a Tropical Whisper

A crab danced with a nearby shoe,
While parrots squawked a tune or two.
The palm tree hat was quite the sight,
But it fell when the wind took flight.

A turtle tried to ride a wave,
But soon discovered it was brave.
With laughter bubbling in the sea,
It slid back home quite happily.

The fish held a conch shell parade,
While snorkelers thought it was handmade.
A dolphin photobombed the scene,
With antics that made the crowd beam.

So here beneath the shade's embrace,
We giggled at each creature's grace.
For fun awaits in every nook,
In each tide pool and cranny's crook.

A Tapestry of Sun-kissed Dreams

A sunburned tourist sought the bar,
But ended up with a coconut star.
It blinked and winked, what a surprise,
While taking selfies with the flies!

Beach towels tangled in a mess,
A picnic turned into a press.
With sand in sandwiches galore,
Who knew lunch could be such a chore?

Seagulls argued over a chip,
While one attempted a daring flip.
The waves cheered on their feathery foes,
As laughter mixed with ocean blows.

And when the sun began to sink,
We gathered 'round for one last drink.
With jokes and jests, our hearts did gleam,
In this land of zany, sun-kissed dreams.

Harmonies of the Secret Bay

Banana boats zoomed with glee,
While frogs croaked in perfect harmony.
A parrot stole a snack or two,
Juicy mango? Yes, that'll do!

The hermit crabs held a race,
Though all were quite the slowpoke case.
Their shells adorned with glitter bright,
As spectators cheered with delight.

A fisherman hummed a silly tune,
While searching for jigs and spoons.
His catch was a boot, oh what a shame,
He proudly claimed it was the aim!

As twilight whispered to the sea,
We laughed 'til dawn, so wild and free.
For every moment here was gay,
In the melodies of the secret bay.

Rhythms of the Forgotten Isle

A monkey on a skateboard flew,
Chasing coconuts that rolled askew.
With giggles echoing through the trees,
While crabs hosted their karaoke spree!

An iguana posed for a pic,
Unbothered by the camera's click.
With shades and a hat, quite stylish too,
It claimed the beach as its own venue.

Pineapples tumbled down the hill,
While everyone laughed, trying for a thrill.
A coconut fell, and what a roar!
As heads turned to see, "Who's on the floor?"

In dance we twirled; oh what a sight,
As rhythms filled the fading night.
In every twinkle, laughter flowed,
Among the beats of the isle's abode.

Melodies of a Coastal Mirage

Seagulls squawk with silly glee,
While crabs dance on the sandy spree.
Waves giggle as they race ashore,
Telling secrets lost in ocean's lore.

A beach ball bounces, laughter flies,
Dancers slip as seagulls size.
With popsicles melting in the sun,
A race for ice cream, all in fun!

Sun hats wobble, kite tails sway,
Wind's a prankster in bright array.
Catch that frisbee, oh what a feat,
It lands in your soda, how sweet!

When twilight whispers, the fun won't end,
Glow sticks shimmer, and night we'll send.
With starry winks and crabs that stroll,
Tonight's a laughter, that's our goal!

The Lighthouses of Lost Stories

A lighthouse winks on tipsy rocks,
Its keeper wears mismatched socks.
With tales of pirates and fish so tall,
The seagulls giggle, they know it all.

One bulb shines bright, the other dims,
As locals craft some sea shanty hymns.
Whispers of mermaids and treasure maps,
Every tale grows with cheeky chaps.

Sandy footprints lead to nowhere,
Where narrow-minded crabs start their dare.
Spectacles held up by fragile pride,
While jellyfish join the joyride.

When the moon's a crank, and stars get loud,
Flickering lights dance with the crowd.
In this lighthouse of stories galore,
We find the magic, and laugh even more!

Bastions of Castle Rocks

On craggy cliffs, a castle stands,
With guards made out of seaweed bands.
A dragon snores, dreaming of pie,
While fish in armor march on by.

Lost in reverie, the knights play chess,
With crabby threats, they can't digress.
Riding tides on plastic steeds,
Off to fetch their salty beads.

A prince gets tangled in seaweed's clutch,
His castle helm caused way too much.
With laughter echoing through the night,
They stage a duel, all in delight.

When dawn arrives, the jesters grin,
For every castle holds room for sin.
In laughter's light and a splash of cheer,
These bastions, oh so dear!

Patches of Heaven in Aquamarine

Under skies of vivid hue,
Turtles ride on waves of blue.
They wear sunglasses, looking so cool,
While dolphins dance in shimmering pool.

Picnic blankets under palm trees sway,
As frogs challenge their hops today.
In sun hats flipped, the laughter stacks,
While snacks fly high on joyful tracks.

A beachcomber slips on wet sand,
Seashells tumble as giggles expand.
With juice boxes spilled, all in good cheer,
Their smiles sparkle like the sea dear.

As the sun sets, they share a pie,
And count the stars that light the sky.
In patches of heaven, oh what a scene,
Life is funny, and so serene!

Dance of the Moon on Silvery Waves

The moon spins round like a disco ball,
Fish join in, giving it their all.
Starfish tap dance on the coral stage,
While crabs moonwalk, full of rage.

Jellyfish float with their fancy flair,
Chasing seafoam without a care.
Octopus grooves, limbs in a twist,
All in a whirl, how could we resist?

Seahorses shimmy, so slick and spry,
While turtles stop to laugh and sigh.
Underwater parties never cease,
As bubbles burst, bringing us peace.

The night is alive, a sparkling sight,
Under moonlight, everything feels right.
In this watery world, joy flows and sways,
A rhythmic delight, the ocean plays.

Chasing Shadows Between the Tides

A crab got lost in the swirling sand,
Chasing his shadow, thought he was grand.
Waves rolled in with a chuckle so deep,
'You can't catch what's yours, back to sleep!'

Seagulls swoop low with a cheer and a squawk,
Cracking jokes as they strut on the rock.
No need to worry, they said with a laugh,
'Just don't ask the fish for their photograph!'

With a splash of humor and a wink from the tide,
Even the barnacles join in for the ride.
Laughter echoes down to the clams in their beds,
'What's so funny? Wish we had legs instead!'

The shadows play tag as the sun says goodnight,
Making silly shapes in the soft moonlight.
From laughter to giggles, they twist and they glide,
Chasing each other, they dance with great pride.

When Waves Kiss the Sandy Embrace

Sandy toes giggle as waves rush ashore,
Salty kisses leaving us wanting more.
A flip-flop flops off, it starts to protest,
'Oh no! Not the water, I'm not ready yet!'

Seashells laugh, all polished and bright,
Shells cracking jokes, what a silly sight!
A crab says, 'Why do we scramble on sand?'
To catch quick snacks that are getting out hand!'

Waves gather round for a quirky parade,
Spraying all beachgoers, who laugh and get laid.
Umbrellas dance as a wind makes them twirl,
While sandcastles wobble, waiting to hurl!

As twilight settles, the humor survives,
Under the stars, where every joy thrives.
With laughter in hearts and sand in our hair,
We dance with the waves, without a care.

Stories Carried by the Ocean Mist

The ocean whispers secrets in a breezy tone,
While dolphins giggle, playing on their own.
'What did the sea say to the boat?' asks one,
'You're all afloat, but I'm having more fun!'

As mist rolls in, it tells stories untold,
Of pirates and treasures, glittering gold.
But seagulls mock loudly and won't let it slide,
'All those tall tales need a better guide!'

Crabs hold a conference on the damp land,
Arguing over who's the best in the band.
They strum on their shells, a crustacean tune,
While the waves just laugh, 'We're all here for the moon!'

So if you ever wander with eyes on the sea,
Remember the tales of humor and glee.
With laughter in currents and jokes in each mist,
The ocean's a stage, none shall be missed!

www.ingramcontent.com/pod-product-compliance
Lightning Source LLC
Chambersburg PA
CBHW072222070526
44585CB00015B/1449